MY LOVE
IS LIKE...

POETRY FOR LOVERS

EDITED BY LUCY CAPON

PENGUIN BOOKS

PENGUIN BOOKS

Published by the Penguin Group, Penguin Books Ltd, 27 Wrights Lane, London w8 5tz, England. Penguin Books USA Inc., 375 Hudson Street, New York, New York 10014, USA. Penguin Books Australia Ltd, Ringwood, Victoria, Australia. Penguin Books Canada Ltd, 10 Alcorn Avenue, Toronto, Ontario, Canada m4v 3b2. Penguin Books (NZ) Ltd, 182–190 Wairau Road, Auckland 10, New Zealand · Penguin Books Ltd, Registered Offices: Harmondsworth, Middlesex, England · Copyright © Penguin Books Ltd. This edition published 1996. Set in 10/12pt Monotype Bembo. Typeset by Rowland Phototypesetting Ltd, Bury St Edmunds, Suffolk. Printed in England by Clays Ltd, St Ives plc

CONTENTS

A Red Red Rose

O my Luve's like a red, red rose,
  That's newly sprung in June;
O my Luve's like the melodie
  That's sweetly play'd in tune. –

As fair art thou, my bonie lass,
  So deep in luve am I;
And I will love thee still, my Dear,
  Till a' the seas gang dry. –

Till a' the seas gang dry, my Dear,
  And the rocks melt wi' the sun:
I will love thee still, my Dear,
  While the sands o' life shall run. –

And fare thee weel, my only Luve!
  And fare thee weel, a while!
And I will come again, my Luve,
  Tho' it were ten thousand mile!

ROBERT BURNS

Sonnet XLIII, from The Portuguese

How do I love thee? Let me count the ways.
I love thee to the depth and breadth and height
My soul can reach, when feeling out of sight
For the ends of Being and ideal Grace.
I love thee to the level of every day's
Most quiet need, by sun and candlelight.
I love thee freely, as men strive for Right;
I love thee purely, as they turn from Praise.
I love thee with the passion put to use
In my old griefs, and with my childhood's faith.
I love thee with a love I seemed to lose
With my lost saints, – I love thee with the breath,
Smiles, tears, of all my life! – and, if God choose,
I shall but love thee better after death.

ELIZABETH BARRETT BROWNING

The First Day

I wish I could remember the first day,
First hour, first moment of your meeting me;
If bright or dim the season, it might be
Summer or winter for aught I can say.
So unrecorded did it slip away,
So blind was I to see and to foresee,
So dull to mark the budding of my tree
That would not blossom yet for many a May.
If only I could recollect it! Such
A day of days! I let it come and go
As traceless as a thaw of bygone snow.
It seemed to mean so little, meant so much!
If only now I could recall that touch,
First touch of hand in hand! – Did one but know!

CHRISTINA ROSSETTI

First Love

I ne'er was struck before that hour
  With love so sudden and so sweet,
Her face it bloomed like a sweet flower
  And stole my heart away complete.
My face turned pale as deadly pale,
  My legs refused to walk away,
And when she looked, what could I ail?
  My life and all seemed turned to clay.

And then my blood rushed to my face
  And took my eyesight quite away,
The trees and bushes round the place
  Seemed midnight at noonday.
I could not see a single thing,
  Words from my eyes did start –
They spoke as chords do from the string,
  And blood burnt round my heart.

Are flowers the winter's choice?
   Is love's bed always snow?
She seemed to hear my silent voice,
   Not love's appeals to know.
I never saw so sweet a face
   As that I stood before.
My heart has left its dwelling-place
   And can return no more.

JOHN CLARE

from *The Hunting of Cupid*

What thing is love? for, well I wot, love is a thing.
It is a prick, it is a sting,
It is a pretty thing;
It is a fire, it is a coal,
Whose flame creeps in at every hole;
And as my wit doth best devise,
Love's dwelling is in ladies' eyes:
From whence do glance love's piercing darts
That make such holes into our hearts;
And all the world herein accord
Love is a great and mighty lord,
And when he list to mount so high,
With Venus he in heaven doth lie,
And evermore hath been a god
Since Mars and she played even and odd.

GEORGE PEELE

Love

Love is a sickness full of woes,
   All remedies refusing;
A plant that with most cutting grows,
   Most barren with best using.
        Why so?
More we enjoy it, more it dies;
If not enjoyed, it sighing cries,
        Heigh ho!

Love is a torment of the mind,
   A tempest everlasting;
And Jove hath made it of a kind
   Not well, nor full, nor fasting.
        Why so?
More we enjoy it, more it dies;
If not enjoyed, it sighing cries,
        Heigh ho!

SAMUEL DANIEL

The Passionate Shepherd to His Love

Come live with me and be my Love,
And we will all the pleasures prove
That hills and valleys, dales and fields,
Or woods or steepy mountain yields.

And we will sit upon the rocks,
And see the shepherds feed their flocks
By shallow rivers, to whose falls
Melodious birds sing madrigals.

And I will make thee beds of roses
And a thousand fragrant posies;
A cap of flowers, and a kirtle
Embroidered all with leaves of myrtle.

A gown made of the finest wool
Which from our pretty lambs we pull;
Fair-linèd slippers for the cold,
With buckles of the purest gold.

A belt of straw and ivy-buds
With coral clasps and amber studs:
And if these pleasures may thee move,
Come live with me and be my Love.

The shepherd swains shall dance and sing
For thy delight each May morning:
If these delights thy mind may move,
Then live with me and be my Love.

CHRISTOPHER MARLOWE

An Argument

I've oft been told by learned friars,
   That wishing and the crime are one,
And Heaven punishes desires
   As much as if the deed were done.

If wishing damns us, you and I
   Are damned to all our heart's content;
Come, then, at least we may enjoy
   Some pleasure for our punishment!

THOMAS MOORE

To His Coy Mistress

Had we but world enough, and time,
This coyness, Lady, were no crime.
We would sit down and think which way
To walk and pass our long love's day.
Thou by the Indian Ganges' side
Shouldst rubies find: I by the tide
Of Humber would complain. I would
Love you ten years before the Flood,
And you should, if you please, refuse
Till the conversion of the Jews.
My vegetable love should grow
Vaster than empires, and more slow;
An hundred years should go to praise
Thine eyes and on thy forehead gaze;
Two hundred to adore each breast;
But thirty thousand to the rest;
An age at least to every part,
And the last age should show your heart;
For, Lady, you deserve this state,
Nor would I love at lower rate.

    But at my back I always hear

Time's wingèd chariot hurrying near;
And yonder all before us lie
Deserts of vast eternity
Thy beauty shall no more be found,
Nor, in thy marble vault, shall sound
My echoing song: then worms shall try
That long preserved virginity,
And your quaint honour turn to dust,
And into ashes all my lust:
The grave's a fine and private place,
But none, I think, do there embrace.

Now therefore, while the youthful hue
Sits on thy skin like morning dew,
And while thy willing soul transpires
At every pore with instant fires,
Now let us sport us while we may,
And now, like amorous birds of prey,
Rather at once our time devour
Than languish in his slow-chapt power.
Let us roll all our strength and all
Our sweetness up into one ball,
And tear our pleasures with rough strife
Thorough the iron gates of life:
Thus, though we cannot make our sun
Stand still, yet we will make him run.

ANDREW MARVELL

Aubade

Stay, O sweet, and do not rise,
The light that shines comes from thine eyes;
The day breaks not, it is my heart,
Because that you and I must part.
　　Stay, or else my joys will die,
　　And perish in their infancy.

ANON

An Apology for Having Loved Before

They that never had the use
Of the grape's surprising juice,
To the first delicious cup
All their reason render up;
Neither do, nor care to know,
Whether it be best or no.

So they that are to love inclined
Swayed by chance, not choice, or art,
To the first that's fair, or kind,
Make a present of their heart;
'Tis not she that first we love,
But whom dying we approve.

To man, that was in the evening made,
Stars gave the first delight,
Admiring, in the gloomy shade,
Those little drops of light;

Then at Aurora, whose fair hand
Removed them from the skies,
He gazing toward the east did stand,
She entertained his eyes.

EDMUND WALLER

from *Paradise Lost*

How can I live without thee, how forgo
Thy sweet Converse and Love so dearly join'd,
To live again in these wild Woods forlorn?
Should God create another Eve, and I
Another Rib afford, yet loss of thee
Would never from my heart; no no, I feel
The Link of Nature draw me: Flesh of Flesh,
Bone of my Bone thou art, and from thy State
Mine never shall be parted, bliss or woe.

JOHN MILTON

To One in Paradise

Thou wast that all to me, love,
  For which my soul did pine –
A green isle in the sea, love,
  A fountain and a shrine,
All wreathed with fairy fruits and flowers,
  And all the flowers were mine.

Ah, dream too bright to last!
  Ah, starry Hope! that didst arise
But to be overcast!
  A voice from out the Future cries,
'On! on!' – but o'er the Past
  (Dim gulf!) my spirit hovering lies
Mute, motionless, aghast!

For, alas! alas! with me
  The light of Life is o'er!
  No more – no more – no more –
(Such language holds the solemn sea
  To the sands upon the shore)
Shall bloom the thunder-blasted tree,
  Or the stricken eagle soar!

And all my days are trances,
    And all my nightly dreams
Are where thy grey eye glances,
    And where thy footstep gleams –
In what ethereal dances,
    By what eternal streams.

EDGAR ALLAN POE

She Walks in Beauty

She walks in beauty, like the night
　Of cloudless climes and starry skies;
And all that's best of dark and bright
　Meet in her aspect and her eyes:
Thus mellowed to that tender light
　Which heaven to gaudy day denies.

One shade the more, one ray the less,
　Had half impaired the nameless grace
Which waves in every raven tress,
　Or softly lightens o'er her face;
Where thoughts serenely sweet express
　How pure, how dear their dwelling place.

And on that cheek, and o'er that brow,
　So soft, so calm, yet eloquent,
The smiles that win, the tints that glow,
　But tell of days in goodness spent,
A mind at peace with all below,
　A heart whose love is innocent!

LORD BYRON

Eurydice to Orpheus

A PICTURE BY LEIGHTON

But give them me, the mouth, the eyes, the brow!
Let them once more absorb me! One look now
   Will lap me round for ever, not to pass
Out of its light, though darkness lie beyond:
Hold me but safe again within the bond
   Of one immortal look! All woe that was,
Forgotten, and all terror that may be,
Defied, – no past is mine, no future: look at me!

ROBERT BROWNING

My true love hath my heart, and I have his,
By just exchange, one for the other given.
I hold his dear, and mine he cannot miss:
There never was a better bargain driven.
His heart in me, keeps me and him in one,
My heart in him, his thoughts and senses guides:
He loves my heart, for once it was his own:
I cherish his, because in me it bides.
His heart his wound receivèd from my sight:
My heart was wounded with his wounded heart,
For as from me, on him his hurt did light,
So still methought in me his hurt did smart:
    Both equal hurt, in this change sought our bliss:
    My true love hath my heart and I have his.

SIR PHILIP SIDNEY

'My True Love Hath My Heart
and I Have His'

None ever was in love with me but grief.
　　She wooed me from the day that I was born;
She stole my playthings first, the jealous thief,
　　And left me there forlorn.

The birds that in my garden would have sung,
　　She scared away with her unending moan;
She slew my lovers too when I was young,
　　And left me there alone.

Grief, I have cursed thee often – now at last
　　To hate thy name I am no longer free;
Caught in thy bony arms and prisoned fast,
　　I love no love but thee.

MARY COLERIDGE

Love ran with me, then walk'd, then sate,
Then said *'Come, come! it grows too late:'*
And then he would have gone ... but ... no ...
You caught his eye; he could not go.

W. S. LANDOR

Farewell ungrateful traitor,
    Farewell my perjured swain,
Let never injured creature
    Believe a man again.
The pleasure of possessing
Surpasses all expressing,
But 'tis too short a blessing,
    And love too long a pain.

'Tis easy to deceive us
    In pity of your pain,
But when we love you leave us
    To rail at you in vain.
Before we have descried it,
There is no bliss beside it,
But she that once has tried it
    Will never love again.

The passion you pretended
    Was only to obtain,
But when the charm is ended
    The charmer you disdain.

Your love by ours we measure
Till we have lost our treasure,
But dying is a pleasure,
   When living is a pain.

JOHN DRYDEN

Like the Touch of Rain

Like the touch of rain she was
On a man's flesh and hair and eyes
When the joy of walking thus
Has taken him by surprise:

With the love of the storm he burns,
He sings, he laughs, well I know how,
But forgets when he returns
As I shall not forget her 'Go now'.

Those two words shut a door
Between me and the blessed rain
That was never shut before
And will not open again.

EDWARD THOMAS

So shoots a star as doth my mistress glide
At midnight through my chamber, which she makes
Bright as the sky when moon and stars are spied,
Wherewith my sleeping eyes amazëd wake:
Which ope no sooner than herself she shuts
Out of my sight, away so fast she flies:
Which me in mind of my slack service puts;
For which all night I wake, to plague mine eyes.
Shoot, star, once more! and if I be thy mark
Thou shalt hit me, for thee I'll meet withal.
Let mine eyes once more see thee in the dark,
Else they, with ceaseless waking, out will fall:
    And if again such time and place I lose
    To close with thee, let mine eyes never close.

JOHN DAVIES OF HEREFORD

'Give me Women, Wine, and Snuff'

Give me Women, Wine, and Snuff
Until I cry out, 'Hold, enough!'
You may do so sans objection
Till the day of resurrection;
For, bless my beard, they aye shall be
My belovèd Trinity.

JOHN KEATS

My life closed twice before its close –
It yet remains to see
If Immortality unveil
A third event to me

So huge, so hopeless to conceive
As these that twice befell.
Parting is all we know of heaven,
And all we need of hell.

EMILY DICKINSON

To Caroline

I

You say you love, and yet your eye
　No symptom of that love conveys,
You say you love, yet know not why
　Your cheek no sign of love betrays.

II

Ah! did that breast with ardour glow,
With me alone it joy could know,
Or feel with me the listless woe,
　Which racks my heart when far from you.

III

Whene'er we meet, my blushes rise,
　And mantle through my purpled cheek,
But yet no blush to mine replies,
　Nor do those eyes your love bespeak.

IV

Your voice alone declares your flame,
And though so sweet it breathes my name,
Our passions still are not the same,
　Though Love and Rapture still are new.

V

For e'en your lip seems steep'd in snow,
  And, though so oft it meets my kiss,
It burns with no responsive glow,
  Nor melts, like mine, in dewy bliss.

VI

Ah! what are words to love like mine,
Though uttered by a voice divine,
I still in murmurs must repine,
  And think that love can ne'er be true,

VII

Which meets me with no joyous sign;
  Without a sigh which bids adieu:
How different is that love from mine,
  Which feels such grief when leaving you.

VIII

Your image fills my anxious breast,
Till day declines adown the West,
And when, at night, I sink to rest,
  In dreams your fancied form I view.

IX

'Tis then, your breast, no longer cold,
  With equal ardour seems to burn,
While close your arms around me fold,
  Your lips my kiss with warmth return.

X

Ah! would these joyous moments last!
Vain HOPE! the gay delusion's past;
That voice! — ah! no, 'tis but the blast,
  Which echoes through the neighbouring grove!

XI

But, when *awake*, your lips I seek,
  And clasp, enraptur'd, all your charms,
So chills the pressure of your cheek,
  I fold a statue in my arms.

XII

If thus, when to my heart embrac'd,
No pleasure in your eyes is trac'd,
You may be prudent, fair, and chaste,
  But ah! my girl, you *do not love!*

LORD BYRON

Music, when soft voices die,
Vibrates in the memory –
Odours, when sweet violets sicken,
Live within the sense they quicken.
Rose leaves, when the rose is dead,
Are heaped for the belovèd's bed;
And so thy thoughts, when thou art gone,
Love itself shall slumber on.

PERCY BYSSHE SHELLEY

Echo

Come to me in the silence of the night;
   Come in the speaking silence of a dream;
Come with soft rounded cheeks and eyes as bright
    As sunlight on a stream;
      Come back in tears,
O memory, hope, love of finished years.

O dream how sweet, too sweet, too bitter sweet,
   Whose wakening should have been in Paradise,
Where souls brimfull of love abide and meet;
    Where thirsting longing eyes
      Watch the slow door
That opening, letting in, lets out no more.

Yet come to me in dreams, that I may live
   My very life again though cold in death:
Come back to me in dreams, that I may give
    Pulse for pulse, breath for breath:
      Speak low, lean low,
As long ago, my love, how long ago.

CHRISTINA ROSSETTI

My Dearest Julia

Oh! can or can I not live on,
Forgetting thee, my love forgone?
'Tis true, where joyful faces crowd
And merry tongues are ringing loud,
Or where some needful work unwrought
May call for all my care and thought,
Or where some landscape, bath'd in light,
May spread to fascinate my sight,
Thy form may melt awhile, as fade
Our shades within some welkin shade,
   And I awhile may then live on,
   Forgetting thee, my love forgone.

But then the thrilling thought comes on,
   Of all thy love that's now forgone;
Thy daily toil to earn me wealth,
Thy grief to see me out of health,
Thy yearning readiness to share
The burden of my toil and care,

And all the blessings thou hast wrought
In my behalf by deed and thought.
And then I seem to hear thee calling,
Gloomy fac'd with tear drops falling,
   'Canst thou then so soon live on,
Forgetful of my love forgone?'

WILLIAM BARNES

Love and Jealousy

How much are they deceived who vainly strive,
By jealous fears, to keep our flames alive?
Love's like a torch, which if secured from blasts,
Will faintlier burn; but then it longer lasts.
Exposed to storms of jealousy and doubt,
The blaze grows greater, but 'tis sooner out.

WILLIAM WALSH

Did Not

'Twas a new feeling – something more
Than we had dared to own before,
　　Which then we hid not;
We saw it in each other's eye,
And wished, in every half-breathed sigh,
　　To speak, but did not.

She felt my lips' impassioned touch –
'Twas the first time I dared so much,
　　And yet she chid not;
But whispered o'er my burning brow,
'Oh, do you doubt I love you now?'
　　Sweet soul! I did not.

Warmly I felt her bosom thrill,
I pressed it closer, closer still,
　　Though gently bid not;
Till – oh! the world hath seldom heard
Of lovers, who so nearly erred,
　　And yet, who did not.

THOMAS MOORE

She that Denies Me

She that denies me, I would have;
   Who craves me, I despise:
Venus hath power to rule mine heart,
   But not to please mine eyes.
Temptations offered, I still scorn,
   Denied, I cling them still;
I'll neither glut mine appetite
   Nor seek to starve my will.

Diana, double-clothed, offends –
   So Venus, naked quite.
The last begets a surfeit, and
   The other no delight.
That crafty girl shall please me best
   That 'no' for 'yea' can say,
And every wanton willing kiss
   Can season with a 'nay'.

THOMAS HEYWOOD

Sudden Light

I have been here before,
    But when or how I cannot tell:
I know the grass beyond the door,
    The sweet keen smell,
The sighing sound, the lights around the shore.

You have been mine before, –
    How long ago I may not know
But just when at that swallow's soar
    Your neck turned so,
Some veil did fall, – I knew it all of yore.

Has this been thus before?
    And shall not thus time's eddying flight
Still with our lives our love restore
    In death's despite,
And day and night yield one delight once more?

DANTE GABRIEL ROSSETTI

Upon the Death of Sir Albert Morton's Wife

He first deceased; she for a little tried
To live without him, liked it not, and died.

SIR HENRY WOTTON

A Valediction

If we must part,
   Then let it be like this;
Not heart on heart,
   Nor with the useless anguish of a kiss;
But touch mine hand and say;
'Until tomorrow or some other day,
   If we must part.'

Words are so weak
   When love hath been so strong:
Let silence speak:
   'Life is a little while, and love is long;
A time to sow and reap,
And after harvest a long time to sleep,
   But words are weak.'

ERNEST DOWSON

Alter? When the hills do.
Falter? When the sun
Question if his glory
Be the perfect one.

Surfeit? When the daffodil
Doth of the dew:
Even as herself, O friend!
I will of you!

EMILY DICKINSON

And You, Helen

And you, Helen, what should I give you?
So many things I would give you
Had I an infinite great store
Offered me and I stood before
To choose. I would give you youth,
All kinds of loveliness and truth.
A clear eye as good as mine,
Lands, waters, flowers, wine,
As many children as your heart
Might wish for, a far better art
Than mine can be, all you have lost
Upon the travelling waters tossed,
Or given to me. If I could choose
Freely in that great treasure-house
Anything from any shelf,
I would give you back yourself,
And power to discriminate
What you want and want it not too late,
Many fair days free from care
And heart to enjoy both foul and fair,

And myself, too, if I could find
Where it lay hidden and it proved kind.

EDWARD THOMAS

What Lips My Lips Have Kissed

What lips my lips have kissed, and where, and why,
I have forgotten, and what arms have lain
Under my head till morning; but the rain
Is full of ghosts tonight, that tap and sigh
Upon the glass and listen for reply,
And in my heart there stirs a quiet pain
For unremembered lads that not again
Will turn to me at midnight with a cry.
Thus in the winter stands the lonely tree,
Nor knows what birds have vanished one by one,
Yet knows its boughs more silent than before:
I cannot say what loves have come and gone,
I only know that summer sang in me
A little while, that in me sings no more.

EDNA ST VINCENT MILLAY

To —*

Time's sea hath been five years at its slow ebb,
   Long hours have to and fro let creep the sand,
Since I was tangled in thy beauty's web,
   And snared by the ungloving of thy hand.
And yet I never look on midnight sky,
   But I behold thine eyes' well memoried light;
I cannot look upon the rose's dye,
   But to thy cheek my soul doth take its flight;
I cannot look on any budding flower,
   But my fond ear, in fancy at thy lips,
And hearkening for a love-sound, doth devour
   Its sweets in the wrong sense: – Thou dost eclipse
Every delight with sweet remembering,
And grief unto my darling joys dost bring.

JOHN KEATS

* A lady whom he saw for some few moments at Vauxhall.

Song

I love the jocund dance,
   The softly-breathing song,
Where innocent eyes do glance,
   And where lisps the maiden's tongue.

I love the laughing vale,
   I love the echoing hill,
Where mirth does never fail,
   And the jolly swain laughs his fill.

I love the pleasant cot,
   I love the innocent bow'r.
Where white and brown is our lot,
   Or fruit in the mid-day hour.

I love the oaken seat,
   Beneath the oaken tree,
Where all the old villagers meet,
   And laugh our sports to see.

I love our neighbours all,
　　But, Kitty, I better love thee;
And love them I ever shall;
　　But thou art all to me.

WILLIAM BLAKE

Remember

Remember me when I am gone away,
   Gone far away into the silent land;
   When you can no more hold me by the hand,
Nor I half turn to go, yet turning stay.
Remember me when no more day by day
   You tell me of our future that you planned:
   Only remember me; you understand
It will be late to counsel then or pray.
Yet if you should forget me for a while
   And afterwards remember, do not grieve:
   For if the darkness and corruption leave
   A vestige of the thoughts that once I had,
Better by far you should forget and smile
   Than that you should remember and be sad.

CHRISTINA ROSSETTI

To Celia

Drink to me only with thine eyes,
   And I will pledge with mine;
Or leave a kiss but in the cup
   And I'll not look for wine.
The thirst that from the soul doth rise
   Doth ask a drink divine;
But might I of Jove's nectar sup,
   I would not change for thine.

I sent thee late a rosy wreath,
   Not so much honouring thee
As giving it a hope that there
   It could not withered be;
But thou thereon didst only breathe,
   And sent'st it back to me;
Since when it grows, and smells, I swear,
   Not of itself but thee!

BEN JONSON

To Mary: It is The Evening Hour

It is the evening hour,
    How silent all doth lie,
The hornèd moon he shows his face
    In the river with the sky.
Just by the path on which we pass,
The flaggy lake lies still as glass.

Spirit of her I love,
    Whispering to me,
Stories of sweet visions, as I rove,
    Here stop, and crop with me
Sweet flowers that in the still hour grew,
We'll take them home, nor shake off the bright dew.

Mary, or sweet spirit of thee,
    As the bright sun shines tomorrow.
Thy dark eyes these flowers shall see,
    Gathered by me in sorrow.
In the still hour when my mind was free
To walk alone – yet wish I walked with thee.

JOHN CLARE

Love is begot by fancy, bred
   By ignorance, by expectation fed,
Destroyed by knowledge, and, at best,
Lost in the moment 'tis possessed.

GEORGE GRANVILLE,
BARON LANSDOWNE

Sonnet XXI, from the Portuguese

Beloved, say again and yet again
That thou dost love me – Though the word repeated
Should seem a cuckoo-song, as thou dost treat it,
Remember, never to the hill & plain,
Valley & wood, without her cuckoo-strain,
Comes the sweet Spring in all her green, completed!
Beloved! – I, amid the darkness greeted
By a doubtful spirit – voice, in the doubt's pain
Cry . . . speak once more . . . thou lovest! Who can fear
Too many stars, though each in heaven should roll . . .
Too many flowers, though each should crown the year? –
Say thou dost love me, love me, love me – toll
The silver iterance! – only minding, dear,
To love me also in silence, with thy soul.

ELIZABETH BARRETT BROWNING

Shall I compare thee to a summer's day?
　Thou art more lovely and more temperate:
Rough winds do shake the darling buds of May,
　And summer's lease hath all too short a date:
Sometime too hot the eye of heaven shines,
　And often is his gold complexion dimmed;
And every fair from fair sometime declines,
　By chance, or nature's changing course untrimmed;
But thy eternal summer shall not fade,
　Nor lose possession of that fair thou owest,
Nor shall death brag thou wanderest in his shade,
　When in eternal lines to time thou growest;
　　So long as men can breathe, or eyes can see,
　　So long lives this, and this gives life to thee.

WILLIAM SHAKESPEARE

READ MORE IN PENGUIN

For complete information about books available from Penguin and how to order them, please write to us at the appropriate address below. Please note that for copyright reasons the selection of books varies from country to country.

IN THE UNITED KINGDOM: Please write to *Dept. EP, Penguin Books Ltd, Bath Road, Harmondsworth, Middlesex UB7 0DA.*

IN THE UNITED STATES: Please write to *Consumer Sales, Penguin USA, P.O. Box 999, Dept. 17109, Bergenfield, New Jersey 07621-0120.* VISA and MasterCard holders call 1-800-253-6476 to order Penguin titles.

IN CANADA: Please write to *Penguin Books Canada Ltd, 10 Alcorn Avenue, Suite 300, Toronto, Ontario M4V 3B2.*

IN AUSTRALIA: Please write to *Penguin Books Australia Ltd, P.O. Box 257, Ringwood, Victoria 3134.*

IN NEW ZEALAND: Please write to *Penguin Books (NZ) Ltd, Private Bag 102902, North Shore Mail Centre, Auckland 10.*

IN INDIA: Please write to *Penguin Books India Pvt Ltd, 706 Eros Apartments, 56 Nehru Place, New Delhi 110 019.*

IN THE NETHERLANDS: Please write to *Penguin Books Netherlands bv, Postbus 3507, NL-1001 AH Amsterdam.*

IN GERMANY: Please write to *Penguin Books Deutschland GmbH, Metzlerstrasse 26, 60594 Frankfurt am Main.*

IN SPAIN: Please write to *Penguin Books S. A., Bravo Murillo 19, 1º B, 28015 Madrid.*

IN ITALY: Please write to *Penguin Italia s.r.l., Via Felice Casati 20, I-20124 Milano.*

IN FRANCE: Please write to *Penguin France S. A., 17 rue Lejeune, F-31000 Toulouse.*

IN JAPAN: Please write to *Penguin Books Japan, Ishikiribashi Building, 2-5-4, Suido, Bunkyo-ku, Tokyo 112.*

IN SOUTH AFRICA: Please write to *Longman Penguin Southern Africa (Pty) Ltd, Private Bag X08, Bertsham 2013.*